T0368561

NINETY FIVE YEARS

Stories and thoughts from two teachers over their lifetimes to help parents.

Elizabeth Wiley MA JD, Pomo Elder

1st Edition

Order this book online at www.trafford.com
or email orders@trafford.com

Most Trafford titles are also available at major online book retailers.

 www.trafford.com

North America & international
toll-free: 844 688 6899 (USA & Canada)
fax: 812 355 4082

Our mission is to efficiently provide the world's finest, most comprehensive book publishing service, enabling every author to experience success. To find out how to publish your book, your way, and have it available worldwide, visit us online at www.trafford.com

ISBN: 978-1-6987-0951-2 (sc)
ISBN: 978-1-6987-0952-9 (e)

Print information available on the last page.

Trafford rev. 11/20/2021

Ninety Five Years of Teaching

Stories and thoughts from two teachers, who over their lifetimes taught more than 95 years, the book is to help parents. teachers, and others know that teaching is about giving someone the gift of loving to learn. AND learning how to survive in the real world without too much loss of self.

1st Edition

INTRODUCTION:

This book started out to be stories about all our years of teaching, and include stories from other teachers. As we drafted, it became what it is....The second volume of this book will be a lot more stories and how we learned to be teachers. We are still learning, and we are retired.

INTRODUCTION:

Our books are written as on ongoing series for high risk youth, veterans, and first responders as well as their parents and those who are raising them.

One of the reasons for starting this series was we, as special needs teachers, as therapists, as Directors of programs and private schools for high risk youth began to recognize how many of the children and youth were children of veterans, grandchildren of veterans, and also first responders.

We then noticed the numbers of minority children and poverty level financial back grounds were the reality for high risk children and youth. We saw children of Mothers who had been as young as NINE at the birth of their child among the high risk students. Whether rich, or poverty level, we saw children of alcohol, sexual, and drug addictions.

We saw children as young as 18 months labeled with an alphabet of mental health disorders, medicated and put into "special schools" where in fact media found they were often warehoused, abused, and not taught at all. Upon seeing a news story about the schools discovered at some of the licensed sites, in which children and teens often did not have desks, or chairs to sit on, let alone proper educational supplies and equipment for special learning program, we joined with others, and designed programs.

We were naive enough to think our work, offered FREE in most cases, would be welcomed especially as we offer it free and all materials paid for through research projects, but, it was NOT valued or wanted.

What? we asked? Why? we asked?

We went back to college and while earning degrees we had apparently NOT needed while working with children of the very rich in expensive private schools, we did research projects to document our findings. To find ways to overcome the problems. Again, our work was NOT valued or wanted.

One of our associates, who had asked many of us to volunteer in a once a month FREE reading program in the local public schools, was held back for almost two years doing paperwork and proving her volunteers, most of them parents of successful children, teens and adults, could read a first five years book and teach parents how to read those books to their own children. She was a Deputy United States Prosecutor, and had recruited friends from all levels of law enforcement, child and family services, education and volunteer groups that served children and families.

None the less, we continued our work, met a fabulous and expensive Psychiatrist who was building his own server system and the first online education project after creating a massive and encompassing medical examination study guide for graduate medical students to assist them in passing global and national medical examinations for licensing.

We worked with a team of citizens and specialists in education who had created a 39 manual project for students, parents and teachers to be able to learn on their own.

This series of books includes ideas, history and thoughts from the students, the parents, and professionals who work with these situations.

Jesus was told by his followers, don't have children wasting your time, and he responded, let the children come.

Our work is to bring children to us, and to those who have the heart and love to develop the uniqueness and individuality of each of God's creations. Many of them are of different religions, and beliefs, and many are atheists but believe fully in the wonder and uniqueness of every human.

To all who have helped and continue to help children and anyone wanting to learn, we thank God and we thank you.

CHAPTER ONE

Teaching: 95 years between two of us, more with our whole staff and Board of Directors

Teaching is about giving away the love of learning, about helping a person find that love of learning, about helping someone else find the way to fulfill their dreams.

The years of just two of our co-founding directors equal ninety-five plus years of teaching and program directing. Special education, education support programs, and family support programs. This book is about how we got many of our ideas, a brief description of those areas of education, and introduction to the ideas of what a parent and/or child is responsible for learning just to get along in our complex society.

One of the most important things to learn is that you do NOT have to be what someone else wants you to be, or what someone else tells you to be (trends, advertising, movies, etc). Learn to just be YOU, and happy being that unique amazing person.

CHAPTER TWO

Passing pre-school interview

Today it is quite possible, in fact, often happens, that a child fails pre-school interviews, is sent to an evaluation, listed with mental problems, medicated and their life and dreams are over.

Make sure your child does not suffer this horror.

Children, from the day they are born, need loving guidance, not everything they want, the minute they want it. A child who can pass a pre-school interview is often asked to sit and talk to an adult.

Make sure your child can sit, not fidget, and talk with and to an adult about whatever it is the adult is asking. The answer does not have to be "right", but the ability to give respect, and focus to the adult is being evaluated for pre-school admission.

PASSING Pre-school interviews

Put plainly, to succeed, even in pre-school a child needs to pass the interview to get into pre-school. There are a lot of programs that you do NOT want your child involved in, Bullying, fighting, racism, gender bias, financial bias are all areas that you do NOT want your child to get involved, either by being a bully, or a victim of bullies.

Currently the general rule is that BOTH involved in any incident are punished. The superior way to deal with these issues is TAUGHT, not just segmented out in interviews and later disposed of by expelling "bad" kids.

Think back, you will remember a certain type of child, they ALWAYS pass the interviews in general type programs. YET, every teacher recognizes this child within an hour in class. This is the child who irritates, and quietly bullies another child until they react, and then shout out "teacher, teacher".

We will discuss the best method for handling this problem in a later chapter.

The interviewer is also going to notice immediately what I call "the kid police" because when confronted by this "helpful" tattle tale, I say "WHO MADE YOU the kid police". More on this in a later chapter as well.

In the interview process, the interviewer is going to ASK the child about being bullied, and about how to resolve the problems.

In the schools that are best for your child (NOT the most expensive, the best)the interviewers are going to talk to you and your child about building better social skills and bullying and being bullied.

In a simple model, there is the concept of I am wonderful, and YOU are wonderful, so let's work this out. This will be discussed in a later chapter, but is a truly important stepping stone to survival, not just in school, but survival in life.

IN a pre-school interview, your child will be observed in the observation part of the orientation for interviews for acceptance to the school. The teachers and Principal are experienced in choosing children who are gong to be successful and make THEM look successful, they are NOT going to choose children that will not fit the program and make them look like failures. THIS IS SAD. A baby is here for us to train, NOT to run our home, and certainly NOT their school.

One of the biggest parts of the interview is what YOU have to say. If you constantly say, MY CHILD doesn't like, or won't, or wants, you are going to tell the school what kind of disrespectful and time wasting parent they would have to deal with, if they accept your child, and they won't.

YOU have just made your child a two or three year old failure.

CHAPTER THREE

Passing pre-school

What, we ask, is there to pass, eat graham crackers, drink pineapple juice, finger-paint? Sit and listen to the teacher read ABC, one two three, and colors related books. Attributes. Color, size, shape.......

How YOU are going to help your child pass pre-school

GO TO THE ORIENTATIONS of more than one pre-school program.

ASK questions: What is the philosophy of the school?

IF the school seems to have a philosophy of train to the test, and get your child out, without critical thinking skills, to have no dreams, and no hope, find another school.

IF the school talks a lot about mental illness in children, and are likely to label your child, find a therapist, further label them, and put them on medications without HOPE for the rest of their lives......find another school.

Children, said my children's pediatrician, who was friends with most of the famous global doctors of his time, do NOT have the neurological capability for mental illness. Every teacher, principal, therapist or social worker for juveniles is now screeching and showing their own weak social and mental skill sets.

CHILDREN for centuries, millennia, have had addicted Mothers, Fathers or both. How many children, in history, if reality were discussed, instead of those perfect people that history attempts to tell us were there always, were born of at least a Mother who drank, sniffed snuff, and possibly a Father who drank since early teens, and also sniffed snuff and smoked the rope and clothing growing plants out in the fields. But they did not seem to have fetal alcohol or fetal drug global pandemics.

IF, thanks to YOUR drug and alcohol abuse, or prescription medication abuse you have a child with some behavioral issues, many teachers, therapists, psychiatrists, and principals have taken the attitude that the child can be salvaged. Honesty is the first step. There are drugs, such as heroin and fentanyl that have not had the academic studies to prove whether the drugs themselves, the poor nutrition and self care of the mothers while pregnant, a bottle of Jack, Jose and whoever else on their favorite beverage list is NOT good pre-natal health. Starving to brag they "only" gained five pounds and had a seven pound baby has to be severely detrimental to the pre-natal development. BUT, today, we blame it all on fetal alcohol syndrome, label the child, and give up hope.

It is hard to look at the reality that most of the children so labeled are PUT ON DRUGS and sent to hopeless lock downs until they are *eighteen. I have seen few small private facilities that DO anything, except rake in the money for "caring" for these children.*

YET, I have seen many teachers, and parents who refused to give up hope on a child often less than three, and through out their lives watched those children grow into great adults, with dreams, the skills to make most of them come true, and a willingness to help others so labeled.

Pre-school is the first place to best address that it just might be possible, that the child that came to you without instructions, does not have the learned skills to be a success enough to get into pre-school. AND admit that maybe you can learn how to turn that around. With the help of hopeful and skilled professionals. Many of these programs are local, parent originated, and FREE. You will be expected to help with fundraisers and volunteer at the program in barn raisers, usually assisted by a large community building project to keep costs and time for labor low.

To prepare your child for pre-school, and pre-school interviews ASK some of the best pre-schools for their suggestions for YOUR CHILD to help get your child ready for the interviews.

ASK for lists of books, and field trips you can take with your family PRIOR to the interviews to help your child pass the interviews...

ASK for online and televised programs to watch and interact with to facilitate for your child to pass the interviews.

A few suggestions to help your child pass pre-school admissions interviews:

READ books to your child. These do not have to be kid books, or pre-school educational books, read YOUR favorite magazines to them, read

YOUR homework to them, online or in a book. Read and write letters, let them be part of both email to family and friends, and also to cards and letters.

THIS is the time to train yourself, along with your child to SEND thank you messages. Especially cards to anyone over fifty. Younger family members "might" be OK with a thank you text, but you and your child need to be aware that thank you cards, letters and in some cases gifts are kind, proper and NEED to be addressed within a day or two of receiving a present, money, or a ride somewhere from relatives.

YOU might be amazed at how kind and receptive your siblings and in laws are to help you out in a pinch, or just pick up your kids from school if you THANK THEM, formally. Thank them often if it is ongoing help. Have your children draw them thank you pictures and do. a chore to earn money to buy them small. gifts. Grandmother are the only people who feel loved and thanked with a package of cute sponges or hand soap for the bathroom. Grandfathers truly appreciate a $20 bill in a thank you card for after school pick up and taking the kids to sports, dance and after school *activities they would otherwise miss due to your job.*

Having the children do chores and earn the money for the gifts and cards makes them even more meaningful, AND teaches your children to be grateful for time and expenditures made for them.

A friend, of a lot of decades of life, and really good manners, was sad, and complaining that her brother had not talked to her for years, and not returned calls. She was convinced to go visit and ASK him what the problem was. He let her have it, he said, are you aware that in almost two decades you have never called me or come by except to ask for money, which you never once sent a thank you for, when I said you do not have to repay it.

When I had cancer, you did not even send me a text asking how I was. It might be best to train our children and ourselves to start to know what good, kind manners are about. It is NOT to sell cards, flowers, candy or texting phones. It IS to remember always to care as much for someone else as we expect them to care for us, and to remember to DO something from time to time for that person.

We have a very wealthy friend, very busy, and with little time, we suggested for his birthday to send donations to HIS favorite charities and send a card or text letting his office executive put them all into a package for his birthday. This is a person who certainly has EVERYTHING, or can purchase it, and is so busy, might just like a day OFF on his birthday. He loved it. He also loved the few, small presents he received, just the right amount.

Pre-School is where children learn to make a present for parents and others that means a lot. I still have a loop of macaroni beads, hand

painted decades ago by one son. A personal,
heartfelt letter from the other after he had
disappointed himself and the family for a short
period. A tiny ceramic cat from one brother,
the ONLY present he ever gave me. HE loved
that I mentioned still having it and cherishing
it in my birthday message to him. I was kind
enough not to mention it was even more special
because it was THE ONLY one he ever gave me.
His wife sent gifts and cards to every family
member, every holiday and event, they are still
in a box, and beloved, but that little cat.....has
a special place in my heart. Children NEED

to learn this young, and how much it means.

This is where your child learns that some actions are good social skills, not just crumpets and tea, useless ceremony.

It may seem rude, but you do NOT want your child to sneeze on the interviewer, or pick her/his nose and rub it on the chair in the office of the Director.

Teach your child WHY it is healthy and polite to use handkerchiefs and paper wipes. Teach your child why it is healthy and polite to put the used paper wipes in the trash, and the used handkerchief in their pocket to take home and put in the laundry basket.

A child going to pre-school NEEDS to know that big boy, or big girl bathrooms are for health and sanitation. Many pre-schools have uni-gender bathrooms to discourage an unhealthy pre-occupation with gender ideas, making them into peeping tom or tomisinas to try and see if everyone is the same or different. If gender is a natural part of each learning day, children do NOT try to peep.

When a child knows WHY, they are much less likely to just do, or not do things that make them *socially disliked. If for no other reason, teach your child to listen, and to chat with others.*

When a child gets to kindergarten without the requisite skills to call their Grandparents and other relatives to say hello, how are you, and LISTEN to what the person has to say, with appropriate response, that child is going to be disliked by other children.

Pre-schools teach these skills, but have to have a place to start. When a pre-school has 1,000 applicants and 100 slots, any child who does not pass all aspects is going to be left out. Again, it is YOUR responsibility to make sure your child has the skills to get into and out of pre-school aptly.

Academics: Many children in high level pre-schools have parents that work in jobs with high academic skills, and read for pleasure. They have parents who communicate by text, email, FB and Twitter because they are busy, and often live far from family and close friends. They do NOT appreciate your child coming in and telling them these phones and computers are to find "I see your butt" pictures.

Many children in advanced pre-schools know what sex is, and keep it in its normal place *for their age. They are well aware that some grown ups molest children, and to watch out and repeat suspicious adults or teens. They will tell their parents if other children show them inappropriate social media posts. You do NOT want to have the FBI show up at your door to find out why your child is showing other children truly objectionable pornography.*

Many people "think" that "men" think about sex every few seconds, NOT unless they are addicted to pornography and/or sex. Children who present inappropriate material to other students can and will be turned over to children's protective services and the courts for evaluation, it is mandatory reporting. NO child is learning these things without a misguided teen or adult, or molester showing them where to find those sites.

If it is on YOUR phone and/or computer, being made available to children YOU may be arrested and tried for a minimum charge of neglect and providing child molesting materials to children. Other parents are really upset and angry at this type of destruction of their children's innocent childhood. While there are a few nations around the world that allow really *young girls to marry, and even have babies, many of the immigrants with these practices have been shocked when arrested, tried, and convicted as pedophiles and put on lifetime sex offenders against children registries.*

There are many age appropriate books about the science of sexuality, if nothing else, consult the school psychologist and find out what the school is teaching. Children in earlier times used to live on farms, or at least have chickens, and ducks and know about eggs, and chicks and ducklings and how they come to be. Children in earlier times often slept in a nursery or the same bed with six to twelve siblings. Older children helped take care of, bathe, and change clothing of younger children. None of the children had the need to wonder what the genitals of the other kids looked like.

Today that is not true. Other parents get really angry and often call the police if your child is asking to see other children's "privates". Those children have been warned to report anyone who attempts to invade their privacy or worse, touch them.

YOUR child has to understand the right of every human to privacy of body. Get appropriate books and go to farms, ranches, and zoos. If your family is one that changes clothes in front of each other, or the other side, NEVER lets anyone see any part of any one else's body, your child needs to understand everyone has equal rights to their at home behavior, but everyone has a right to privacy at school.

You are by now thinking, what has this to do with years of teaching. Most schools do not bother to train teachers to deal with these situations. Many schools have no plan for teaching ALL the children that sex is a normal part of human development, WHEN they are old enough and responsible enough to get a job and care for a baby. That is very clean, not religious, or too liberal for some parents. It leaves all families to work with their own family beliefs, and to respect the beliefs of other families.

Health and self care. Children NEED to know, especially after COVID, that it is necessary to wash your hands before touching your face, or preparing, or eating food. Even the smallest children can understand microscopic bacteria, virus and fungus......but it needs to be presented as health and science, not a scary way to be sure your child develops obsessive compulsive disorders about washing hands, staying healthy, and the possibility of deadly disease.

Small children may NOT have any idea what death is. It depends on their experience with death of close relatives and friends, and how that was handled by the family. It depends on their experience with death of pets and how that is handled. It is NOT necessary to assure your child is afraid to eat because they figure out that plant or animal, something gave up its life to feed us.

CHAPTER FOUR

Passing Kindergarten interviews

Again, what is there to pass, isn't kindergarten where a child learns to learn? Climbs the jungle gym out in the yard, today it might not even be considered PC to call the structure a jungle gym.......Isn't this another place for crackers and peanut butter? Learning to hold hands to cross the street? Finger-painting pictures to hang on the refrigerator.

Not any more.

At a kindergarten interview a child needs to be able to enter a room, sit down, speak directly to an unknown adult, answer questions asked, and ask questions that make sense when asked if she/he has questions during the interview.

A kindergarten may invite children in small groups of four or five to attend class with the students in January as they are preparing the schedules for the fall.

Your child is going to be expected to follow directions about where to sit, to not bother the other students, to participate when asked.

Your child is going to be expected to sit in a group of children and listen as a book is read, NO questions, NO why, why, why? NO, I have to go potty half way through the book. A failure to be capable of sitting in a group listening to a book is often a prescription to the therapist for an alphabet of behavior disorders, medication and already on the NO list for many careers later in life.

YOU are the one responsible to read around your child, to read TO your child, and most kindergarten students accepted into top line kindergartens already can recognize letters and some words.

YOUR child needs to understand WHY we need letters and words. Called attributes your child needs to have a start on colors, shapes and sizes. Numbers. Today a child of five should realize that menus at restaurants have all the food listed, with prices (both words and numbers) and that the numbers relate to money.

One child told her Grandmother to buy something, the Grandmother said she did not have enough money. The child said, OH, just go get some with that card. The Grandmother drily told her that you have to put money in to get money out.

Your child needs to understand that you can NOT just buy everything and let the card pay for it. SHOW them how to add up the prices, add the tax, tell them what tax is about. That we each have a responsibility for the things we, the PEOPLE decide we need and our leaders collect the money, and oversee how it is spent. And we the PEOPLE have a RIGHT to a true account of what those taxes are spent for. Politicians NEED to try to tell a group of five year olds why they take money for certain use, and then use it for something else. It would more than likely lower taxes and make sure we have better oversight for OUR money.

This seems a lot for a five year old, but in today's world, children need a head start, and that does not mean taking math YOU do not understand and being taught to tests that have nothing to do with reality to your family, or to what your child's dreams may be in order for your district to score high points in State and National testing.

When I got to law school, I was told, this is it, you spent four years to get here, had to pass the LSAT (which asked questions I knew the answers to, but never had used, and never have used, such as something about what kind of model a little table was....how do ranch kids know, or care, how do poverty level kids know or care), and now would spend more years studying and in class to take class, and annual tests to finally take another class so we could learn how to pass the Bar, and finally, if we could find someone to hire us, find a law office to teach us how to be a lawyer.

When I worked at a hospital, it was a training hospital, most of those students had been top *of their classes since middle school. Had been in advanced science, math, and biology and physiology since high school. Spent ELEVEN years in college, medical school and applying for internships.....and never touched or spoken to a patient.*

At our law office, even with a three year mandatory work history in a tough law office, we hired lawyers that quit after a week or two, they had done only research and case preparation after THEIR grueling four years of pre- law, and three years of law school, some schools only two years of pre law, and three years of law school....and NEVER talked to a client, or walked around a jail, or court room.

One lawyer, with glowing referrals from her professors, from moot court, from her jobs in law firms, worked one half day seeing clients, and never came back, not even for her check, she asked for it to be mailed. She could not stand the reality of their lives.

The point: let your child be a child and have dreams, let them do what they have to in order to survive and move ahead in the dominant culture of money, academics and laws and rules. It is up to you to help them navigate this rough sea. Coming out the other end, knowing a lot of it makes no sense, and some does, and it just is. You have to choose your battles in life. It can't be sitting quietly to listen to a little book being read to ALL the kids.

CHAPTER FIVE

Science-hands on and family field trips

This is part of being able to be successful in all grades, social activities, and yet to maintain your own individual self.

As noted above, what you do with your family is going to harm, or help your child in school, at all levels. From pre-school to graduate graduation.

Loving to learn is the most important part.

Learning how the academic world demands you learn and not to bother fighting it until you are through and can help someone else NOT go through the boring useless hell you went through is important, for your child, and for you to model.

Modeling and talking to your child is MUCH more important than whatever someone is texting you while you are driving, or yakking about on the phone that you have coming through the car radio........Tell them why other drivers are dangerous. Tell them why it is important for them to be quiet and attentive while driving.

My sons had been well indoctrinated to the idea that if an emergency came up, they had to be quiet enough to hear me say something, AND act fast to do what I asked them to do.

One day while driving, I said, I am going to stop, run over to that store, tell the man to call the fire department and tell them this car is on fire. They were under six. They did exactly as asked. My engine had caught fire, as just happened from time to time with that type of car. There were no cell phones, with Siri to ask to call the fire department.

Another time, one of my sons, again very young, said, MOM, be calm, but stop, and pull on the other side of the street as you stop. HE had seen a baby crawl out a door and gate, and under a car, HE knew it was going to end up right under my wheels if I did not move away from MY side of the street and stop.

Lucky for that kid and family he was NOT playing video games in the car seat.

I taught ALL my students, Scouts, and field trip kids to BE QUIET, read a book, or sit and look *out the windows to see their city and where we were going on the bus or in a car. I taught ALL of them to listen and do what was asked in an emergency.*

Many a bus driver thanked me for this extra teaching. Many a parent thanked me when they avoided an accident because they could HEAR and concentrate on driving instead of being distracted by the chaos going on in the vehicle...

Science Even the smallest child can begin to understand, a human can SEE a vehicle, the vehicle can NOT see the child. A child can stop in a step or two, or turn aside....a vehicle, especially a big one, can NOT stop fast. There are online resources to show the science behind this reality that might save your child's life, whether dashing out into traffic, or later as a new driver.

Field trips of every kind help your child connect to the whole world.

A walk around the block, to a small child, if YOU let them stop, look, listen, smell, touch, is a field trip.

Even a walk around your house or yard.

Little children today, know how to use computers and phones, when your child wants to know WHY, or WHAT, teach them to ask the computer or phone. Seri can help them, but you can also add writing and reading as you help them with this part of making every moment science, math, reading, writing experience and gain of skill.

Many children arrive in kindergarten five years behind other children. BUT, many children are more athletic, have better balance, and maybe are more social than some of those with the academic skills.....we learned in hands on science team projects that with a balanced team, the students balance and teach each other and learn to not just accept others as they are, but to help them become better at some skills so the team can make it.

SPORTS to our program are for balance, fun, health and team building. I developed what I called whacky sports. The teams change at any time I sound the bell. OR a child that is not able for that day to exercise, gets to have the bell and ring it from time to time. ALL children learn ALL positions, and those who are really good at athletics get to teach the others, and those who may be the know it alls of every other subject learn how to learn, and not just hide from others who can do something better than they.

Children who learn to value themselves and each other grow up better equipped to take the reality of life that YOU may not always be the "best", but you still are YOUR best.

Science starts by saying "goodnight sun, good night world" with your child, watching the sunset. Science starts by staring at stars, IF you live in a place where urban light has made the stars invisible, at least once in a while, go to place where you can see stars, point them out to your baby, and toddler and sing say the poem "Starlight, starbright" it can be found online.......and make a wish.

Your child has no idea what a wish is, but you have started the imagination to begin. I wish I have a pizza party with my friends is a start to understanding the physics and dynamics of all science, which appears to be "If you can believe it, you can achieve it". Of course science demands that you then find out the rules of science, and apply them or find new ones to make your dream come true.

A three year old can understand that birds fly, and once humans looked at birds, and had a wish to fly. They invented airplanes, jets, helicopters. Now there are even little jet systems that allow a person to fly. Space travel is becoming more and more like taking an airplane used to be.

Fish swim, deep in the sea. Humans said, I want to go deep in the sea, and submarines were invented. Today you can watch amazing life under the sea, by divers who go down further into the depths, and small drone subs that can bring their own light to show millions of viewers of programs on computer or television what has been unknown to humans.

Horses, no matter how powerful and rich a king, were the only way to get around. Humans said, what if we could ......and invented cars, trucks, busses.

WE now have the duty to harness these creations of humans to stop pollution, land destruction, and the end of wild lands and forests. We can do these things easily.

We met YOUNG, spirited, hopeful scientists that in their wishes see a restored world. A *world which every human, every animal and every plant has rights. They created papers, and gave seminars on how to do this, much of it is available, NOT in twenty, or thirty, or fifty years......for a cost less than the destruction of our world.*

YOU can help your child by getting involved in projects such as THE JANE GOODALL FOUNDATION Roots and Shoots local community projects. Whether on your block, in your child's pre-school, religious or community programs, YOU and your child(ren) can begin to save the earth and to restore the plants, animals, and to make sure everyone HELPS to keep it clean.

THIS brings a question, answered in another chapter about inspiration vs punishment as a great parenting method, a great leadership method.......This is discussed in Chapter 11. While teaching children and teens about the math of crime, the students created a math of pollution and greed and the crimes involved in those realities.

YOU can find a couple of old waste baskets, or trash cans at yard sales, or rolling down the street after a windstorm. YOU can help your child(ren) and their friends talk to the local hardware store experts and find out what is the best (safe for the environment) paint to paint the surface, and have a pizza pot luck with kids and old people on your block. Most hardware stores (or local gardeners who can buy wholesale at the hardware store) will give you a great price on the potting soil. Ask each person to bring a small bag or plastic tub of compost (all the yard and house trash that can be composted safely-look this up online).

Fill the bottom half of your "pot" with compost mixed with dirt, or potting mix. Fill the rest with potting soil. Go online and find a BEE or butterfly and hummingbird mix. OR ask the nursery for six or seven plants (depending on the size of your "butterfly, bee and hummingbird" container. This is a simple exercise that from the age a child in arms can see the plants, or seeds grow, and the bees, butterflies and hummingbirds come to feed when the plants blossom. YOU are setting the stage for your child to learn how to wait......how to dream of what is going to come(go online and to the library and bookstore and read about these small creatures of our earth) and how to be consistent in care of something you are responsible for. YOUR child has learned to find and ask experts.

There is a great cookbook that I used for my sons, nieces, nephews, neighborhood kids, and students for decades. It fits into the movies, books, toys about Winnie the Pooh. Your child will be curious. WHY do Pooh and everyone else love honey so much? YOU read online about honey and tiny children, and YOU ask your own pediatrician if and when YOUR child can eat honey.

When your child learns that butterflies and hummingbirds need the "nector" from flowers to live, buy them hummingbird feeders. GO ONLINE and find out how to safely choose the feeding solution. When in doubt, buy the commercial one. Some forms of raw, or other sugars harm the tiny birds, making it impossible for them to feed and they die. Some white sugars are not processed with safe processing for the tiny birds.

READ about butterflies. The favorite book of many teachers "Caterpiller" found in yard sales, thrift shops and of course bookshops and online book selling corporations shows how caterpillars grow and "become" a butterfly.

How important it is not to bother the little silk bound self made wrapper in which the caterpillar changes into a butterfly. It takes time, just like chicks in their eggs, If humans "help" them, they die or are horribly deformed by too much air that dries them too fast.

THIS teaches your child an amazing thing about science. Study science, but don't bother it. Cameras, drones, under sea drone subs with cameras teach scientists so much more today than the old habits of killing the animals to "learn" about them. MRI and scanners and x rays help in a moment of capture and release with blood tests and chips to track and record the free movement of the animals, fish, birds help us to learn how to better save wild spaces, restore wild spaces and love and honor the land and animals.

Science teaches us to ask not just why, we can learn from records of other scientists, and video of the real plants, seas, and animals taken by others who have left the earth and animals pristine even while studying them closely.

Science also teaches us to ask WHY NOT.

My sister E. used to love to walk around Cal

Tech a long block from our Grandmother's home. She used to look at the students, and wonder what was in their brains. Since we were children, so much has been invented. So many things are becoming better.

Computers when we first saw them were underground, in huge at least block long buildings still seen in old spy or space films. Over our lives, someone in their mind said, WHY NOT make them smaller. Today people have wrist watches that can do all the things those huge computers did and more. Not one of those HUGE computers could instantly tell millions of people their heart rate, their pace as they jogged, or where they had jogged to if they got lost.

YOUR CAR can talk to you and respond to your questions. Ten years ago, someone said, you should not have to hold your cellphone while driving, the car and Siri can help make this easier and safer for all on the road. Help your child think of what might be, and say WHY NOT.

AND HOW.

Science institutes do NOT take the all A students

in math or even science. The institutes are looking for the students who know how to ask WHY and WHY NOT, and create answers with teams. Space, agriculture, every type of travel and vehicle company needs people who can ask WHY and WHY NOT more than they need a person who answer all the math and science on tests, but does not know how to see the missing piece in a problem.....the WHY......and does not have the "dream-ability" to ask WHY NOT and put the pieces together. It is much easier (I worked in the department that did this) to teach the science and math to a WHY and WHY

NOT person than it is to teach imagination and an interest in WHY and WHY NOT to a top test taker.

The FIRST principle that we were trained to teach Directors of science programs, and principals as well as science teachers was: HANDS ON. A brain does not care what it is learning if it does NOT care (or relate) to what it is being asked to deal with.

The SECOND principle is: NOTHING in science is true. This teaches the WHY and the WHY NOT of science. You can teach this concept to your child. THINK about things, from all *angles before giving an answer. It is very hard for many top students to learn that success is not in grades. YES they got good grades in support math and science to get into the top institutes and university science and engineering programs, YES they have to keep up with the teams to stay and move up in the TEAMS that move ahead.*

BUT, each student needs to have a well developed ability to join the team, to ask the WHY and WHY NOT questions, even if they seem silly or might be disproved. It is not about the answer, it is about the solid premises that might make it work, or not!

Example: What is two plus two.

EVERYONE knows that.

We taught in our orientation programs to train the youngest student to realize the reality, 2 plus 2 does, in most common factors, equal 4.

BUT, everyone needs to learn to at least run the question by their mind .....two what, and two what else.

Learn to ask for definition in the question.

We of course do not recommend that your child

in a regular book driven, test driven math class start spouting the WHY and WHY NOT philosophy and show their complex and critical thinking ability. They do have to learn to walk before they run, dance and spin into the air in joy.

TWO WHAT? Help your child make up thoughts on what those sets of two might be.

TWO KIDS and TWO COOKIES will end up with an answer of two cookie crumb face happy kids.

THIS IS SCIENCE!

ALL great scientists end up being those sweeties, crumbs on face, happy members of teams that have found out the WHY and WHY NOT in a positive way.

The rest are not great, they may know science, they may use science and get paid a lot for that science job, but they are NOT great.

Trendy people say, if you wear this shoe, or that name on your butt, or have the right car, or bicycle, you will be great.

GREAT people say, if you are happy and love yourself and others, and have a great team,

YOU are ALL great.

THAT is science. Scientists all know that their engineering teams are the ones, in the day to day, bolt to bolt, fiber optic thread to fiber optic thread of making dreams reality that have to be teams, and know how to ask WHY and WHY NOT at all stages.

HANDS ON from birth:

YOU are going to learn, maybe learn to ask WHY and WHY NOT with your child.

That too is science.

YOU are going to learn, whether your religious

belief or no religious belief, the world goes around in its path, and the earth, and all the planets, moons, stars and dust particles (some space particles are now being proven to be as big as a moon or earth itself-the Hubble telescope and camera video system is showing us more and more, to scale than ever imagined by the scientists who sent it out into space to see what was to be seen.

DOES it really matter what little dancing on the earth for maybe 100 years brains have to say on the matter? That also is SCIENCE.

It also is GOD, for the reality of Science is that

there is NO ONE ANSWER, WHY and WHY NOT are always there, no matter how certain a team of scientists may be about something. WHY does one group of people get to tell everyone else what to believe, one way or the other. WHY NOT get along, and share, and love and have a happy world. Whether God, or no God, it would probably work better and if yes GOD, probably make that entity a lot happier with humans.

This IS a sensitive subject. DECIDING to love one another and disagree on some subjects is also Hands On Science. Because scientists have to work in teams, with other scientists, with engineers, with production factories, with real humans as part of the reality, scientists have to learn how to talk about differences and come to good conclusions. Their conclusions might be wrong, and not work, the saying "back to the drawing board" is how scientists move on, do not just keep hating, and wanting revenge. NOT getting the problem resolved, the dream up and working for many.

A part of the volunteer work I did was with the department of Diversity. Many students come into huge institutes and universities with

THEIR dream, THEIR ideas, and no social or team skills. Many cultures only know "be the best one, OR ELSE". Students who always got the 4.0 and Plus are dismayed and have to be taught to handle that ALL the other students are 4.0 and Plus and no more grades. Pass or get help and pass is the norm. It was what we taught in diversity programs for depressed, and even suicidal students from other cultures. Team work to them meant compromise with the inferiors. That is a hard lesson to learn after years of hard school work while the other kids were out on TEAMS learning sports, and doing community projects and asking WHY or WHY NOT and accomplishing great things.

SPORTS and COMMUNITY are HANDS ON SCIENCE.

CHAPTER SIX

Hands on math

Hands on math starts long before pre-school interviews, let alone learning to write numbers and then how to add, subtract, multiply, divide, and on to higher math.

DO YOU have any idea of what negative zero is? Your child better, or math, science and technology are going to be a failure for your child. Look up negative zero and see if you can find a definition in real life, in your own home.

IF you have more than one child, or if your child brings a small friend home, YOU are going to know the meaning of negative zero.

Look it up online. NOW give yourself a hands on lesson in negative zero.

HANDS ON FRACTIONS

before your child brings those piles of little papers to you, whining that they can NOT do them, or before your child drags you to that dreaded math homework on the computer, begin to teach the hands on math at an early age.

Two two year olds can learn fractions, division. YOU can learn big lesson. Suggestion: put in your ear buds and turn up the volume.

Give those two, or three, or four, or how ever much noise and anger you can put up with, ear buds in, volume up to max......a cake. A pizza, an easily cut candy bar.

Children appear to grow into stingy and hands on math somewhere at the earliest age they see another child getting one more crumb, or drop, or penny of anything.

Note: this exercise works really well for teaching the value of coins, and bills, and how to divide them evenly.

One child gets to decide how many pieces of whatever it is that needs to be divided.

Another child gets to put marks on the item to divide it

Another child gets to cut the actual pieces

Another child gets to give out the pieces.

This does work with just two children, the tasks just go back and forth.

YOU are going to get a lesson in the policy of the four major financial systems. IT is not going to be quiet, or pretty.

Go online, you can find resources for hands on science and math.

Buy play money. Bills and coins. AND an old gift card disguised as a credit, and/or debit card.

Buy weights, this can be a simple kitchen scale from a thrift or housewares shop.

Let your child learn to read the weight on packages, and weigh the products to see if they are the same as you were charged for at the market check out.

BOTH reading and writing become real when your child wants something . Give them a LIST, help them one letter at a time to write down what it is, and then begin the habit of checking the prices. Reading, writing, and math are now hands on.

An important part of math is to open a future business and education fund for your child. Many credit unions have special scholarship and college funds that give higher interest, and special program membership if the contributions are kept up regularly. $10 a week for 18 years is not a lot of money at once, but it IS a lot when kept for those years with a determined amount of every holiday gift is included.

Many children have special religious, cultural holiday, or coming of age celebrations at ages 13 to 15. These used to be to raise a dowery, or help build a base for buying land and/or a business for a young person. These celebrations, often in the poorest of families, that celebrate with potluck meals, family band playing, or family DJ handling the music raise huge amounts *of money when each relative and friend gifts the teen with $10 or more. Wealthy families often spend more than $100,000 for a one day cerebration. If they spent just $75,000 and put the $25,000 and all gift money into an existing scholarship and/or business fund that rewards the young person and teachers them how to make best use of their money gives a young person an amazing start in life.*

At a celebration in the large facility often rented out for private celebrations across the street from our stable, we heard the loudspeaker assisted speech by the father of a young man from another country that at age ten required a father to hold a celebration to give his son a smoother path to adulthood. Today in America, we learned afterwards, these celebrations are held for both girls and boys equally.

Part of this celebration is the preparation by the young person to learn to make the most of the gifts, and to honor ALL who have given them. They learn, using these gifts for drugs, expensive clothings, other over priced material items or illegal activities that put the family to shame is NOT OK, and should these antics occur, the trust may be expanded to be monitored by an elder, a law firm or bank executor to pay bare living costs to prevent the person from becoming a further shame to the family by needing to be supported by public or private funds not set aside for that purpose.

CHAPTER SEVEN

Reading

When your child gets to pre-school, your child will barely be up with other children if they have a concept that reading is more than something that used to exist before texting.

Parents need to read around their children, whether magazines or newspaper, or online sources, Parents need to read what interests them. Read their interests TO the children to share the reading, but also to share the WHY of reading.

Parents may NOT have been taught to love reading in their childhood. In many countries the only education possible is taught by vicious and often very violent persons. Learning to love reading, or love learning is very difficult, if not impossible in those situations.

Parents often were not supported at home in any learning. No safe place (not necessarily quiet, many people read with LOUD music playing, or in busy parks or on busy beaches)to read, or study in the home was often the reality for parents. Give this gift to your children. A reading corner may be as simple as a beanbag chair on a little rug or even towel where YOU can read to your child(ren) and/or read your material while they read their material.

Many parents get together at the beginning of each school year to work with charities and community volunteers, (including middle and high school students) to make sure every child and teen in the entire district has a knapsack with pencils, pens, erasers, paper to draw on, a sketch book, crayons and/or colored pencils. Age appropriate scissors, a stapler, staple remover, and a variety of clips, glue, and tape. This is a portable homework station.

Each child needs to write a thank you to the community and volunteers for the knapsack and make a pledge to take good care of the materials. If by chance they have too many, most schools and many classes doing this project find "sister/brother schools" in other nations that are honored if they have ONE set for the entire school.

Once our United Nations community program gathered all the left over materials at our public schools, which at that time provided the entire "homework/schoolwork" box to each student at no cost. The children donated washed and cleaned up knapsacks, filled them with as much as possible for their sister/brother school, raised the postage or delivery cost and sent along a little disposable camera WITH a postage paid envelope to send back to the school. The school. would develop the pictures in pairs, and send one set back to the school.

We received a letter, obviously written by a young young person. Tear stains on the paper. We sent the letter with a parent to every classroom in our public/private school program to let them know the sorry of this child, and a request for our forgiveness.

The letter said that the small set of crayons we had sent were so appreciated by all the students (pictures of all ages enjoying the crayons were hand drawn and included from other students) but this sad little student had pressed too hard, and the thin (no one had thought to send a second set of the thicker, younger student crayons used by early art educators)crayon, he told the color, and drew a picture of the broken crayon, had snapped in half. Though the teacher had tried to tape it back together, the student was heart broken to have treated our gift with disrespect and to have dishonored and harmed the other students who all carefully used this box of crayons so carefully.

OUR students, across the city, all ages, were shocked. They had NO idea of children who had to share ONE box of crayons not with another student, or their class, but the whole school. They were shocked to find that ALL the students attended the same school, those in class using the desks and books with care, those outside trying to be as quiet as possible so as not to disturb the learning of others.

OUR students suggested they have a fundraiser,

they said, let's help out the Scouts, who were selling cookies at that time. The students decided if everyone brought in cans and bottles and a couple of parents with trucks turned them in for cash, they could buy some BIG boxes of many more colors, and some boxes of the thick, child crayons, and the money to send them to their sister/brother school. They all signed the we forgive you, you are a kid, but you helped US to be more careful of all we have by your letter.

OUR students decided to have a special day each month, to go to yard sales and buy books, clean their rooms, and donate the many used books they had. Parents asked the city library and the school libraries if they had books to donate. THEY DID! After city book sales, many books were left over!

They even thought of another fundraiser to get money to buy several copies of the paperback books sold at school every few months and ask the company if they could ship them to the sister/brother school for less than it would cost students trying to mail them in regular mail. One of the fathers was in the military, and asked, could the military planes deliver the boxes of books. The answer was: If you can carry them on to the plane, and off the plane, the answer is YES.

Some of the students said, HEY maybe their older students can translate the books into our language, and they will send us a copy in THEIR language. This will help them raise money by our selling the translated books in OUR schools. Many school libraries said, YES, we are interested in books about the many cultures that share the world, and those that have members who have come to America.

The libraries said, we would LOVE translated books for reading days.

When we work together, for the best of all, good things happen.

CHAPTER EIGHT

Writing

Writing is a lot more than learning the alphabet, today many districts do not even teach cursive, to be successful in the higher levels of education and business, your child IS going to have to know cursive and how to spell a lot better than texting wr u ?

YOU can find arguments on both sides for not teaching cursive. Many teachers feel the sensory motor aspects of learning cursive writing helps *students brains develop to better comprehend what they read better. The researchers have not had the interest or the money to fund this research to find out if it is scientifically supported. BUT, sometimes those who teach, know more than those who study teachers.*

CHAPTER NINE

Teaching other kids

If your child is well ahead in class, and anyone starts saying skip a grade, say NO, and ask that your child help others kids catch up. Teaching others with patience and to learn how to enjoy and be successful themselves is the best thing your child can learn, NOT how to be ahead of everyone else. NO ONE likes you if you are ahead.....

Many a child has been touted as a prodigy, yet they grow up to be socially inept. In science, medical, and legal programs someone started to notice that many of the prodigy students did not even know how to say "Good morning, how are you" and actually care and listen to the response in a proper manner.

During hands on science programs ALL children were included in teams. No one had set a goal of team building, it just happened, was noted, and then noted that the students themselves, rather than bully, or withdraw began to work together.

CHAPTER TEN

Physical Education

Physical Education is a lot more than athletic ability: Physical education includes a healthy attitude towards nutrition, treats ONCE in while, and exercise for health for a lifetime.

The understanding of genetics, and WHY some kids have to be much more careful of sugar, white carbs, and fried foods will help your child NOT be THE fat kid, or the sick kid, or the young person who gets type one, or type two diabetes. The idea that all body types are beautiful is a long harsh life walk from bringing your child up to think that fat is beautiful and good nutrition and exercise are not MORE important for larger body types than skinny ones.

Some DO have skinny body types, they are not better, or less than round genetic body types, but just plain fat, or just plain starved children and teens are not healthy or mentally sound. Teach your child to have good nutrition and exercise by having them yourself.

Physical education includes dental care. The

smallest child needs to see a dentist at least once a year. Every school district NEEDS to make arrangements with every dentist practicing in their city, or learning to be a dentist in nearby universities to make sure that every child is seen by a dental hygienist at least every six months, and if needed can be referred to a dentist for follow up.

EVERY girl needs to understand that IF she chooses to be a Mother, even if she is going to give the child up for adoption, she needs to have proper pre-natal nutrition, exercise and an obstetrician to make sure her child gets the *best possible chance at a good healthy life.*

WOMEN, whether young and not wanting to "show" or adults, who try to go about bragging they only gained five pounds and had a seven pound baby are risking the lifelong health of the baby. Many of these women have children with lifelong dental problems, bone problems and often type one diabetes. The scientific studies have not been done to prove this, but most of us have several friends who either had poor nutrition because of financial problems, or simply did not eat, or binge/purged, or had undisclosed anorexia while pregnant.

Globally, it is our responsibility to make sure every human gets a good start. This is not about abortion, or birth control, it is about once a woman knows she is pregnant, she takes care of the baby she is carrying. It is up to society to make sure (we have DNA today) that ALL men who father children take care of them.

Whether sperm donors, or the sperm banks that make a fortune from creating new lives, someone needs to make sure pregnant women are properly cared for and have proper nutrition.

This is not about free anything.....it is about having sense. How many people lose days of work, or have to resign from jobs where the employer spent hundreds of thousands of dollars in time and education, training because the employee has early onset diabetes, dental problems that often lead to heart problems, obesity and other problems from lack of proper maternal health CARE.

Many countries provide pregnancy mentors to facilitate for pregnant women to have these needs met. AFTER the birth many countries have visiting nurse systems that visit ALL new mothers and babies. It does not matter if you are a child of the richest person in a country if your Mother had post-natal depression and does not feed or take care of you properly and with love.

EDUCATION and healthcare systems NEED to make sure every child is educated before age ten (yes, we have nine year old Mothers around the world, some countries even younger when adult men are allowed to marry young girls) about human sexuality and the responsibility for possible new life.

Again this is NOT about abortion or anyone's religious beliefs, it is about the right of someone who is going to be born, or has just been born to be taken care of properly. Selfishly, it is going to save money on mental health and physical health care costs in the future.

WOMEN who have a child while testing at a legal level of drugs or alcohol high enough to damage the fetus need to be warned, get treatment or get sterilized.

There is no excuse for humans, or for the fathers, or mothers of children born with severe health and emotional problems caused by a father who uses a drug or alcohol addicted woman and gets her pregnant, or a woman who does not use birth control along with her drugs and drinking to save a child from the often lifelong problems of her addictions.

This is not about a brave new world big brother system forcing sterilization, it is about rich or poor, educated or not, making sure women and men understand that if you have sex, and produce a new person, you have state required minimal responsibilities. If you can't afford the one child because you spend your money on drugs and drinking, you can't afford more children to be harmed both mentally and physically by your irresponsible attitude and actions.

One of our Social Workers is often called in by military and smaller counties around the country to deal with issues regarding this type of irresponsible parenting. One child she was called in to protect was heard crying in a basement by neighbors. The police could not find anyone responsive to their knocks, so broke down the door. They found a toddler, a small child and a BABY in the basement, locked from the outside. Food, some type of animal kibble had been set out on newspaper and a bucket of water left.

The mother it was found was on welfare, had been tested and put on disability for being legally mentally retarded. Yet no one had given her daily child care support services. In the end, she came home, dropped off, PREGNANT AGAIN, by a young man the police instantly arrested. He was a high level officer at a nearby base, often deployed, and thought taking this woman to take care of HIS needs away from HER squalling, filthy children was OK.

He came from a wealthy family, had a good career, and "everyone" knew it had to not be him. DNA knew better. ALL of those children were HIS. He did not support, or care for his own children and had to have known this woman locked them in that basement to go off with him.

Luckily for the children HIS parents decided that rather than public scandal, they would own the children and since their Mother was being sent to prison, house them and get them a program to help them overcome their horrible beginnings. Of course, once the court had ordered the program, our friend heard no more. Most of this type of case is never heard about. It is not unique.

The soldiers in many countries have sex with women and knowing full well those countries do NOT accept mixed race children, they just leave when their deployment is up.

Our friend was asked to help identify and place the children as Americans. They were identified by social workers, doctors, religious leaders in other countries who ran the orphanages in which the children are often dumped into a "safe" box at night, so the family is not shamed and the Mother does not have to be killed by her father, uncle or brothers, which IS the cultural practice in many of those countries.

HealthCARE includes knowing about the rights of children and how to set up systems that make sure "someone" cares.

We all have miserably failed at protecting the children. Teachers, Principals, other parents, foster care agencies.......we NEED to do better.

One day a class of probation teens came to our stables for a special three hour program. We are very aware this three hours is the only chance these kids are going to ever have to get their situation straight, heal, and move on.

I had noticed that two sisters had really dry, untaken care of hair, that their knees and elbow showed no one had oiled or put lotion on their skin in years. I come from a race that has these issues as well, so notice this problem. I asked the girls if they needed oil, or lotion, we could make sure it was supplied to them. They had no idea.

Then they told me that they took care of their mother since a long ago traffic accident left her in a wheelchair and severely brain damaged.

The probation officer who brought big groups of riders out was shocked. He went back and through their files, no teacher, no social worker, no anyone paid by the system to "care" for these children had even noticed that from a young age, two small girls were taking care of themselves. One teacher did notice their clothing was wrinkled and a "dirty" color. She noted it in a file. She did NOT even ask to find out these two small girls were doing the laundry themselves. Putting ALL the clothing together in washer, then dryer. It looked like it, but that teacher did NOTHING to see what the problem might be.

Did their Mom need a few more dollars for the laundry room in the apartments? Did they not have enough money for soap for more loads. Did their Mom not know that clothing needed to be separated and when dry folded, not left in the baskets. If that teacher had bothered to find out, she would have found that these two small girls were doing it all themselves, the best they could figure out.

They said from other children they had learned not to ask for help, because they would get put in foster homes, and though disabled, their Mom would be put in jail and charged with child neglect.

WHAT are we paying for in child "care" systems.

Maybe with a child care helper, twice a week to help them learn how to properly wash and care for clothing and the house, and with a nurse two or three times a week to care for their Mother, these two girls at early teenage, would not have turned to whatever crime they had committed to get a few extra dollars to care for their Mom. Probation was able to change their situation and since they were old enough to live with assistance two or three times a week they did not have to go to foster homes.

Health "care" includes asking ourselves, and

those who get paid to care for children, disabled, and seniors to do the job they are paid to do. I know it is possible because my Mom was a social worker and later a Deputy of Child Adoptions and Foster care and DID her job, not just paperwork. I did NOT understand or honor my Mother at that time with her career, but did know she worked hard to help families that had no support, no help as our family all had each other. I now honor her work, it often left her apart from her friends, she was on call 24/7 for the foster children. She changed the laws by pushing the State and Federal government to allow foster and group home directors to sign for medical care for the young clients. Before, without my Mom, or another Deputy there, NO medical care, even WITH her there, both she, and the lead doctor had to sign for the child to have care, and then get a judge to OK it.

CHAPTER ELEVEN

The Math of Crime

This project started decades ago with juveniles in lock down probation camps. We taught them that no matter HOW great it might look, being a criminal does NOT pay.

Today, around the world there are silent criminals, hiding behind those that do the actual crimes. The criminals NEED to understand they are just stooges, and no amount of money can pay for the destruction and death they do

FOR someone who does NOT respect or care for them.

Today, around the world, there are silent criminals, those who hide behind their positions in society, or lawyers who "get them off", but in the end, the destruction to our justice systems, and to the rights of ALL people around the world are not worth the money they make. Research some of these people, you will find one woman sold out America for $48 million dollars, that is her net worth. Over the years of her career, she has stolen more property, taken more lives than most armies in the world, and *destroyed the principles of our country. For what amounts to less than $1 Million a year! She could have made more money buying a tee shirt and jogging pants factory and having fundraisers to make sure every person in the world has at least ONE outfit of warm, new clothing in their life. Even if she made $1 per person, it would be over $6.5 BILLION dollars. and everyone would honor her work to serve God and equality.*

Just in the small personal crime level, talk to your child:

I had a student that had started in drugs. His parents came to the school to ask for help. I asked him why he had started drugs. He said he wanted a motorcycle, and his parents would not let him have one. I asked him to find the motorcycle he wanted, to add in insurance, repairs, and gas costs. To figure out how many days until he turned eighteen. To divide the cost by the days. He was surprised to find the cost was less than the cigarettes, beer and drugs he was starting to use . We had him sign a commitment, with his parents, that on his eighteenth birthday, if he had saved up that money, he could have the motorcycle.

We discussed ways he could make the money instead of stealing from parents, and relatives. We discussed how much it was going to cost, maybe his life, if the people he robbed shot him to death, or put him in a wheelchair for the rest of his life. This young man found a motorcycle shop that would let him start a few hours a week, and hang out to learn how to take care of a motorcycle when he got one. In the long run, he decided to spend the money on college, to learn more about business to help run that shop, and one day own his own. He was able to realize the cost of a new motorcycle was not his new dream, and he could purchase used ones from the shop at a discount.

Stealing: we had a first offender workshop in which kids learned to do the math and business plans for they lives to make the same, or more money than they were going to make with crime.

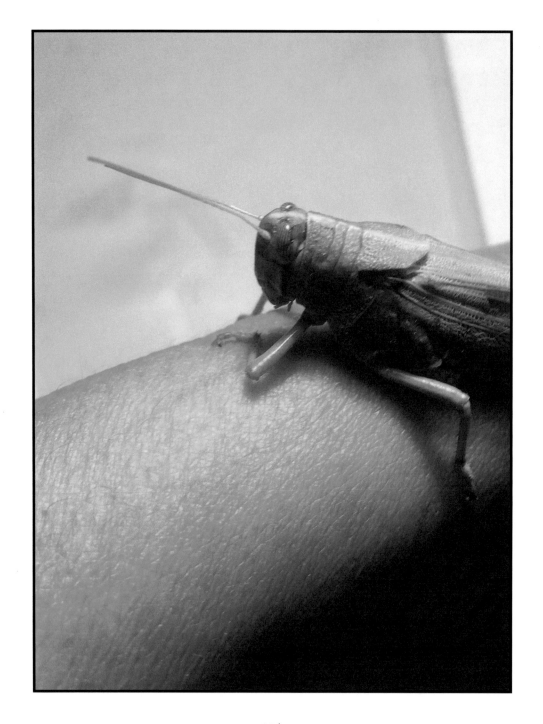

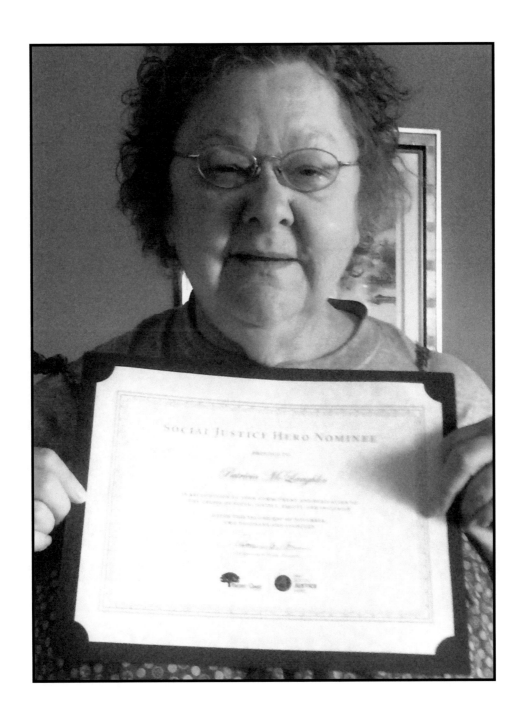

CHAPTER TWELVE

CLOSING: This book is about YOU. and your child. About helping all of us learn about and with each other.

All of us are teachers, all of us are learning at all times. We can close it out, but what we may be learning is to be not living our lives to the full, just sitting around waiting for whatever it is that we are waiting for, instead of learning and living our lives to the fullest.

Closing:

This book is part of a major education project. Elizabeth Wiley Development Center was a Masters' Degree project exploring and researching, asking parents, and students how to best increase their own educational success. As noted in the bio the teachers credited with the stories and materials are only a tiny part of mostly anonymous professionals looking for better ways for students, and parents to take control of the educational process for learning for the fun of it, and also to navigate the wild seas of constantly changing academic requirements to meet your dreams. and goals in modern global business. Sometimes you, and your children just have to accept that it is best to get that degree, that business license and make enough money to hire the level of lawyers it will take to reduce the burden for the next seven generations. Other times it may be in your best interest to talk to professionals, and find the least amount of paper to go and do what it is you want to do, help others.

As noted in this book, there are great programs that in the past have attempted to teach people to teach themselves and their children to deal with the dominant money culture as well as be happy and successful individually. Boy Scouts, Girl Scouts, Camp Fire, Pathways, are ALL books, they are online courses, ALL of these programs want parents to be part of the learning experience. Many parents never got the opportunity to learn how to be their own best self, and help their own dreams come true, to look at reality, prepare for it, and make sure you, your family and others are prepared, and survive many types of crisis in life.

There has been a lot of fear about your kids will get molested in school, religious, and community organizations. NOT if you are there WITH your children. If you think you are going to get a $16 a year babysitter, your CHILD is at risk. ALL public programs, foster care, probation, juvenile rehabilitation programs have their OWN licensed and bonded, background checked professionals present and participating in all of these activities.

Due to divorce, my sons did not have a Dad to move on from Cubs, to Boy Scouts, most of the adults in the local troops were members of my own church, many professionals working at the hospital where I was employed. I petitioned and was allowed to BE their Mom and Dad, since that was our reality, and did many of the activities. My sons, and ALL the youth in our programs were trained in the "youth protection" program. Once this was piloted to be a national mandatory program for every child to be taught to be safe. ALL of those who put these programs together worked with professionals to build a training program for parents to teach in all public and private school programs, This program taught children and teens, even many adults how to be safe in the huge urban reality so many of us live in, as internet moved into our lives, online protection was added to every class.

At the end of each class, I would ask the group, about different persons, ...

What if.......questions.....

What if your best friend's Dad or Mom, or Aunt comes and says, OH, your parents have an emergency, and asked me to pick you up, take you to my house, they will pick you up there.....

The kids ALL say yes.....even after having just taken an interactive workbook driven class on how to be safe.

The answer is ASK the adult you are with to call my Mom or Dad and make sure this is OK.

Some people might get offended, but less adults will get offended by asking for a moment to make sure, than the huge numbers of people who are in divorces, family fights over inheritance or some other family feud and is going to take the child, or children to get revenge, or leverage in a situation.

One horrifying story from a private school was the Aunt came to pick up her niece and nephew. She was NOT on the agreed list to pick up the kids. When the parents came to pick up the kids, they were told, their Aunt picked them up. They asked why. They called the Aunt. SHE had not picked up the kids. Those kids were never seen again their Dad was a Prosecutor, and someone out for revenge had picked up those children.

Divorce is a huge issue in the safety of children. A parent on drugs, or mentally ill may take the children and when pushed into a corner, murder them and commit suicide.

MAKE sure your children are safe, and make sure YOU go over youth protection with your child. IF a person bothers them on the street, make sure they AlWAYS know, go to the nearest STORE and plead for the police to be called.

IF someone tries to kidnap your child in a public place, they NEED to know to get calm, and put their legs and arms out stiff as possible, and flop all their body weight to make it harder to carry them, all the time saying loudly, HELP ME, THIS IS NOT MY PARENT, I AM BEING KIDNAPPED.

People say, OH, it might scare kids. We live in a real world, if we lived in old days of dinosaurs, we would teach our children, stay away from those big feet, and when you see those huge meat eaters, get in a cave it can not get into........children will follow YOUR lead, if you teach them, bleach is not a good afternoon drink, or spit out your toothpaste, it is NOT healthy if you swallow it. THEY learn, and they are not traumatized. Trucks, busses and cars do NOT have eyes, just because you see them, does NOT mean it's driver sees you....and it take at least 10 feet for every 10 miles of speed for a vehicle to stop. DO NOT walk or ride your bike, or later drive in front of vehicles that are moving. This is not traumatizing, it is reality. Kidnappers, molesters, mentally ill and sex trafficking are all real, as real as Dinosaurs once were, and as real as wild life in areas where you are visiting wild life. National Parks are NOT zoos. ZOOS are not petting farm animal parks. The life you save may be your child's.

Our form of education is based on reality, and teaching children and teens to enjoy life, NOT be fearful and anxious, but to be safe.

Other books in our programs:

Closing:

All of our group of books, and workbooks contain some work pages, and/or suggestions for the reader, and those teaching these books to make notes, to go to computer, and libraries and ask others for information to help these projects work their best.

To utilize these to their fullest, make sure YOU model the increased thoughts and availability of more knowledge to anyone you share these books and workbooks with in classes, or community groups.

Magazines are, as noted in most of the books, a wonderful place to look for and find ongoing research and information. Online search engines often bring up new research in the areas, and newly published material.

We all have examples of how we learned and who it was that taught us.

One of the strangest lessons I have learned was walking to a shoot in downtown Los Angeles. The person who kindly told me to park my truck in Pasadena, and take the train had been unaware that the weekend busses did NOT run early in the morning when the crews had to be in to set up. That person, being just a participant, was going much later in the day, taking a taxi, and had no idea how often crews do NOT carry purses with credit cards, large amounts of cash, and have nowhere to carry those items, because the crew works hard, and fast during a set up and tear down and after the shoot are TIRED and not looking to have to find items that have been left around, or stolen.

As I walked, I had to travel through an area of Los Angeles that had become truly run down and many homeless were encamped about and sleeping on the sidewalks and in alleys. I saw a man, that having worked in an ER for many years I realized was DEAD. I used to have thoughts about people who did not notice people needing help, I thought, this poor man, this is probably the most peace he has had in a long time. I prayed for him and went off to my unwanted walk across town. As I walked, I thought about myself, was I just heartless, or was I truly thinking this was the only moment of peace this man had had for a long time and just leaving him to it. What good were upset neighbors, and police, fire trucks and ambulances going to do. He was calmly, eyes open, staring out at a world that had failed him while alive, why rush to disturb him now that nothing could be done.

I did make sure he was DEAD. He was, quite cold rigid.

I learned that day that it is best to do what a person needs, NOT what we need.

Learning is about introspection and grounding of material. Passing little tests on short term memory skills and not knowing what it all means is NOT education, or teaching.

As a high school student, in accelerated Math and Science programs, in which I received 4.0 grades consistently, I walked across a field, diagonally, and suddenly all that math and science made sense, it was not just exercises on paper I could throw answers back on paper, but I realized had NO clue as to what it all really meant.

OTHER BOOKS by this author, and team

Most, if not all, of these books are written at a fourth grade level. FIrst, the author is severely brain damaged from a high fever disease caused by a sample that came in the mail, without a warning that it had killed during test marketing. During the law suit, it was discovered that the corporation had known prior to mailing out ten million samples, WITHOUT warnings of disease and known deaths, and then NOT telling anyone after a large number of deaths around the world started. Second, the target audience is high risk youth, and young veterans, most with a poor education before signing into, or being drafted into the military as a hope Many of our veterans are Vietnam or WWII era.

Maybe those recruiting promises would come true. They would be trained, educated, and given chance for a home, and to protect our country and its principles. Watch the movies Platoon, and Born on the Fourth of July as well as the Oliver Stone series on history to find out how these dreams were meet.

DO NOT bother to write and tell us of grammar or spelling errors. We often wrote these books and workbooks fast for copyrights. We had learned our lessons about giving our material away when one huge charity asked us for our material, promising a grant, Instead, we heard a couple of years later they had built their own VERY similar project, except theirs charged for services, ours were FREE, and theirs was just for a small group, ours was training veterans and others to spread the programs as fast as they could.. They got a Nobel Peace prize. We keep saying we are not bitter, we keep saying we did not do our work to get awards, or thousands of dollars of grants....but, it hurts. Especially when lied to and that group STILL sends people to US for help when they can not meet the needs, or the veterans and family can not afford their "charitable" services. One other group had the nerve to send us a Cease and Desist using our own name. We said go ahead and sue, we have proof of legal use of this name for decades. That man had the conscience to apologize, his program was not even FOR veterans or first responders, or their families, nor high risk kids. But we learned. Sometimes life is very unfair.

We got sued again later for the same issue. We settled out of Court as our programs were just restarting and one of the veterans said, let's just change that part of the name and keep on training veterans to run their own programs. Smart young man.

Book List:

DRAGON KITES and other stories:

The Grandparents Story list will add 12 new titles this year. We encourage every family to write their own historic stories. That strange old Aunt who when you listen to her stories left a rich and well regulated life in the Eastern New York coastal fashionable families to learn Telegraph messaging and go out to the old west to LIVE her life. That old Grandfather or Grandmother who was sent by family in other countries torn by war to pick up those "dollars in the streets" as noted in the book of that title.

Books in publication, or out by summer 2021

Carousel Horse: A Children's book about equine therapy and what schools MIGHT be and are in special private programs.

Carousel Horse: A smaller version of the original Carousel Horse, both contain the workbooks and the screenplays used for on site stable programs as well as lock down programs where the children and teens are not able to go out to the stables.

Spirit Horse II: This is the work book for training veterans and others interested in starting their own Equine Therapy based programs. To be used as primary education sites, or for supplementing public or private school programs. One major goal of this book is to copyright our founding material, as we gave it away freely to those who said they wanted to help us get grants. They did not. Instead they built their own programs, with grant money, and with donations in small, beautiful stables and won....a Nobel Peace Prize for programs we invented. We learned our lessons, although we do not do our work for awards, or grants, we DO not like to be ripped off, so now we copyright.

Reassessing and Restructuring Public Agencies; This book is an over view of our government systems and how they were expected to be utilized for public betterment. This is a Fourth Grade level condemnation of a PhD dissertation that was not accepted be because the mentor thought it was "against government" .. The first paragraph noted that a request had been made, and referrals given by the then White House.

Reassessing and Restructuring Public Agencies; TWO. This book is a suggestive and creative work to give THE PEOPLE the idea of taking back their government and making the money spent and the agencies running SERVE the PEOPLE ;not politicians. This is NOT against government, it is about the DUTY of the PEOPLE to oversee and control government before it overcomes us.

Could This Be Magic? A Very Short Book. This is a very short book of pictures and the author's personal experiences as the Hall of Fame band VAN HALEN practiced in her garage. The pictures are taken by the author, and her then five year old son. People wanted copies of the pictures, and permission was given to publish them to raise money for treatment and long term Veteran homes.

Carousel TWO: Equine therapy for Veterans. publication pending 2021

Carousel THREE: Still Spinning: Special Equine therapy for women veterans and single mothers. This book includes TWELVE STEPS BACK FROM BETRAYAL for soldiers who have been sexually assaulted in the active duty military and help from each other to heal, no matter how horrible the situation. publication pending 2021

LEGAL ETHICS: AN OXYMORON. A book to give to lawyers and judges you feel have not gotten the justice of American Constitution based law (Politicians are great persons to gift with this book). Publication late 2021

PARENTS CAN LIVE and raise great kids.

Included in this book are excerpts from our workbooks from KIDS ANONYMOUS and KIDS JR, and A PARENTS PLAIN RAP (to teach sexuality and relationships to their children. This program came from a copyrighted project thirty years ago, which has been networked into our other programs. This is our training work book. We asked AA what we had to do to become a real Twelve Step program as this is considered a quasi twelve step program children and teens can use to heal BEFORE becoming involved in drugs, sexual addiction, sexual trafficking and relationship woes, as well as unwanted, neglected and abused or having children murdered by parents not able to deal with the reality of parenting. Many of our original students were children of abuse and neglect, no matter how wealthy. Often the neglect was by society itself when children lost parents to illness, accidents or addiction. We were told, send us a copy and make sure you call it quasi. The Teens in the first programs when surveyed for the outcome research reports said, WE NEEDED THIS EARLIER. SO they helped younger children invent KIDS JR. Will be republished in 2021 as a documentary of the work and success of these projects.

Addicted To Dick. This is a quasi Twelve Step program for women in domestic violence programs mandated by Courts due to repeated incidents and danger, or actual injury or death of their children.

Addicted to Dick 2018 This book is a specially requested workbook for women in custody, or out on probation for abuse to their children, either by themselves or their sexual partners or spouses. The estimated national number for children at risk at the time of request was three million across the nation. During Covid it is estimated that number has risen. Homelessness and undocumented families that are unlikely to be reported or found are creating discussion of a much larger number of children maimed or killed in these domestic violence crimes. THE most important point in this book is to force every local school district to train teachers, and all staff to recognize children at risk, and to report their family for HELP, not punishment. The second most important part is to teach every child on American soil to know to ask for help, no matter that parents, or other relatives or known adults, or unknown adults have threatened to kill them for "telling". Most, if not all paramedics, emergency rooms, and police and fire stations are trained to protect the children and teens, and get help for the family.. PUNISHMENT is not the goal, eliminating childhood abuse and injury or death at the hands of family is the goal of all these projects. In some areas JUDGES of child and family courts were taking training and teaching programs themselves to HELP. FREE..

Addicted to Locker Room BS. This book is about MEN who are addicted to the lies told in locker rooms and bars. During volunteer work at just one of several huge juvenile lock downs, where juveniles who have been convicted as adults, but are waiting for their 18th birthday to be sent to adult prisons, we noticed that the young boys and teens had "big" ideas of themselves, learned in locker rooms and back alleys. Hundreds of these young boys would march, monotonously around the enclosures, their lives over. often facing long term adult prison sentences.

The girls, we noticed that the girls, for the most part were smart, had done well in school, then "something" happened. During the years involved in this volunteer work I saw only ONE young girl who was so mentally ill I felt she was not reachable, and should be in a locked down mental health facility for help; if at all possible, and if teachers, and others had been properly trained, helped BEFORE she gotten to that place, lost in the horror and broken of her childhood and early teen years.

We noticed that many of the young women in non military sexual assault healing programs were "betrayed" in many ways, by step fathers, boyfriends, even fathers, and mothers by either molestation by family members, or allowing family members or friends of parents to molest these young women, often as small children. We asked military sexually assaulted young women to begin to volunteer to help in the programs to heal the young girls and teens, it helped heal them all.

There was NOTHING for the boys that even began to reach them until our research began on the locker room BS theory of life destruction and possible salvaging by the boys themselves, and men in prisons who helped put together something they thought they MIGHT have heard before they ended up in prison.

Americans CAN Live Happily Ever After. Parents edition.One

Americans CAN Live Happily Ever After. Children's edition Two.

Americans CAN Live Happily Ever After. Three. After Covid. This book includes "Welcome to America" a requested consult workbook for children and youth finding themselves in cages, auditoriums on cots, or in foster group homes or foster care of relatives or non-relatives with NO guidelines for their particular issues. WE ASKED the kids, and they helped us write this fourth grade level workbook portion of this book to help one another and each other. Written in a hurry! We were asked to use our expertise in other youth programs, and our years of experience teaching and working in high risk youth programs to find something to help.

REZ CHEESE Written by a Native American /WASP mix woman. Using food, and thoughts on not getting THE DIABETES, stories are included of a childhood between two worlds.

REZ CHEESE TWO A continuation of the stress on THE DIABETES needing treatment and health care from birth as well as recipes, and stories from Native America, including thoughts on asking youth to help stop the overwhelming numbers of suicide by our people.

BIG LIZ: LEADER OF THE GANG Stories of unique Racial Tension and Gang Abatement projects created when gangs and racial problems began to make schools unsafe for our children.

DOLLARS IN THE STREETS, ghost edited for author Lydia Caceras, the first woman horse trainer at Belmont Park.

95 YEARS of TEACHING:

A book on teaching, as opposed to kid flipping

Two teachers who have created and implemented systems for private and public education a combined 95 plus years of teaching talk about experiences and realities and how parents can get involved in education for their children. Included are excerpts from our KIDS ANONYMOUS and KIDS JR workbooks of over 30 years of free youth programs.

A HORSE IS NOT A BICYCLE. A book about pet ownership and how to prepare your children for responsible pet ownership and along the way to be responsible parents. NO ONE needs to own a pet, or have a child, but if they make that choice, the animal, or child deserves a solid, caring forever home.

OLD MAN THINGS and MARE'S TALES. this is a fun book about old horse trainers I met along the way. My husband used to call the old man stories "old man things", which are those enchanting and often very effective methods of horse, pet, and even child rearing. I always said I brought up my children and my students the same as I had trained horses and dogs......I meant that horses and dogs had taught me a lot of sensible, humane ways to bring up an individual, caring, and dream realizing adult who was HAPPY and loved.

STOP TALKING, DO IT

ALL of us have dreams, intentions, make promises. This book is a workbook from one of our programs to help a person make their dreams come true, to build their intentions into goals, and realities, and to keep their promises. One story from this book, that inspired the concept is a high school kid, now in his sixties, that was in a special ed program for drug abuse and not doing well in school. When asked, he said his problem was that his parents would not allow him to buy a motorcycle. He admitted that he did not have money to buy one, insure one, take proper driver's education and licensing examinations to own one, even though he had a job. He was asked to figure out how much money he was spending on drugs. Wasting his own money, stealing from his parents and other relatives, and then to figure out, if he saved his own money, did some side jobs for neighbors and family until he was 18, he COULD afford the motorcycle and all it required to legally own one. In fact, he did all, but decided to spend the money on college instead of the motorcycle when he graduated from high school. His priorities had changed as he learned about responsible motorcycle ownership and risk doing the assignments needed for his special ed program. He also gave up drugs, since his stated reason was he could not have a motorcycle, and that was no longer true, he COULD have a motorcycle, just had to buy it himself, not just expect his parents to give it to him.

Printed in the United States
by Baker & Taylor Publisher Services